**What people said about Carlos's previous book,
Lessons from Mars: How One Global Corporation
Cracked the Code on High Performance Teamwork
and Collaboration**

Carlos is an iconoclast   dible but
responsible too. Chall   dom of
corporate team building   ..earch-based
alternative that organizat   ..ains can put to work with
immediate positive impact. His tried and tested approach
delivers concrete results while minimizing the need for external
support. He conveys his experience and wisdom in a style that is
informal and accessible, presenting his robust evidence and no
nonsense advice with humor and humility.
Arvi Dhesi, Senior Client Partner, Korn Ferry

There may be no "I" in team, but there is in "informative", "interesting", "innovative", and "insightful" — all apt descriptions
of *Lessons from Mars*. Building on his nearly 30 years in the field,
Carlos Valdes-Dapena takes a hard look at what passes for team
building in the corporate world and finds it wanting. After thoroughly dissecting the ineffective way most companies spend
their money on team effectiveness, this book offers a cogent,
research-based alternative that can be used by anyone managing
groups of people.
Roy Sekoff, Founding Editor, *The Huffington Post*

I have been a participant in the High Performance
Collaboration approach multiple times throughout my time
at Mars and it is not only a fabulous approach, it is essential
if you really want to focus teams. The approach creates
truly proactive and collaborative teams, with a purpose and
crystallized intent at the heart of everything they do, which

in turn accelerates performance.
Ulf Hahnemann, CHRO, A.P Moeller- Maersk

The Mars Framework for High Performance Collaboration is a 21st-century model for work teams to deliver greater value for their organizations. Workers, managers and leaders in any organization can enhance their teams' effectiveness by understanding and applying these essentials, encapsulated in this easy-to-understand unique model — detailed in his book.
Artie Mahal, author of *Facilitator's* and *Trainer's Toolkit and How Work Gets Done: Business Process Management, Basics and Beyond*

With insight born of years of experience and the warmth of a natural storyteller, Valdes-Dapena lets the air out of "teaminess" and gets to the roots of what motivates productive collaboration. I was surprised, heartened and inspired.
Jane Grenier, Creative Brand Story Teller, Braze.com

Teams of cross-functional leaders know they need to collaborate but on what precisely? Who should be involved and when should they collaborate? This is a great new addition to team development literature and is instantly in my rotation of "go to" sources for management development materials.
Quincy Troupe, Sr, VP, Supply Chain, Boston Beer Company

Resilience: Virtual Teams

Holding the Center When You
Can't Meet Face to Face

The *Resilience* Series

Resilience: Virtual Teams

Holding the Center When You Can't Meet Face to Face

Carlos Valdes-Dapena

CHANGEMAKERS
BOOKS

Winchester, UK
Washington, USA

JOHN HUNT PUBLISHING

First published by Changemakers Books, 2020
Changemakers Books is an imprint of John Hunt Publishing Ltd., No. 3 East Street,
Alresford, Hampshire SO24 9EE, UK
office@jhpbooks.com
www.johnhuntpublishing.com
www.changemakers-books.com

For distributor details and how to order please visit the 'Ordering' section on our website.

Text copyright: Carlos Valdes-Dapena 2020

ISBN: 978 1 78904 691 5
978 1 78904 692 2 (ebook)
Library of Congress Control Number: 2020937390

A CIP catalogue record for this book is available from the British Library.

Design: Stuart Davies

UK: Printed and bound by CPI Group (UK) Ltd, Croydon, CR0 4YY
Printed in North America by CPI GPS partners

We operate a distinctive and ethical publishing philosophy in
all areas of our business, from our global network of authors to
production and worldwide distribution.

Contents

This book is for my friends, collaborators, and supporters who insisted that the High Performance Collaboration framework deserved a wider audience in an accessible format. It's also for the hundreds and hundreds who have used the Framework to help their teams, who continue to use it even though they are forced to work apart. I sincerely hope this book provides needed help in this difficult time.

Acknowledgements

This book would not exist without the leadership, passion and guidance of Tim Ward the Publisher of Changemakers Books, and John Hunt, owner of John Hunt Publishing who is managing the production of this series of books.

I could not have met the aggressive deadlines that were part of this project if I didn't already have the basic shape of the book ready and waiting. Thanks to my friends and colleagues, Phyllis Wallin, Celia Harmon and Kris Terry, who last year worked with me to frame out a shorter, more practical version of my previous book *Lessons from Mars*. That outline and some key content formed the skeleton of this work.

Finally, thanks to my wife, Janet Aldrich for her patience while I cloistered myself within our existing pandemic sequestration to devote my time to getting this done. Her spirit and support never flagged.

Foreword: *Resilience In a Time of Crisis*

"What can we do to help?"

In a time of crisis - such as the 2020 COVID-19 pandemic - we all have a natural impulse to help our neighbors. John Hunt, founder of John Hunt Publishing, asked this question of our company, and then offered a suggestion. He proposed producing a series of short books written by experts offering practical, emotional, and spiritual skills to help people survive in the midst of a crisis.

To reach people when they need it most, John wanted to accomplish this in forty days. Bear in mind, the normal process of bringing a book from concept to market takes at least eighteen months. As publisher of the JHP imprint Changemakers Books, I volunteered to execute this audacious plan. My imprint publishes books about personal and social transformation, and I already knew many authors with exactly the kinds of expertise we needed. That's how the *Resilience* series was born.

I was overwhelmed by my authors' responses. Ten of them immediately said yes and agreed to the impossible deadline. The book you hold in your hands is the result of this intensive, collaborative effort. On behalf of John, myself, the authors and production team, our intention for you is that you take to heart the skills and techniques offered to you in these pages. Master them. Make yourself stronger. Share your newfound resilience with those around you. Together, we can not only survive, but learn how to thrive in tough times. By so doing, we can find our way to a better future.

Tim Ward
Publisher, Changemakers Books
May 1, 2020

Introduction: A Whole New World

It's late April. There have been too many chill rains in the Northeast where I live and too few sunny days. Despite that I find myself yearning to be outdoors. In the past 10 days I have only been out of my house three times, each time wearing a face mask and disposable rubber gloves. Two weeks ago my wife and I along with our eldest daughter, her husband and their childcare giver were exposed to someone who later developed a severe upper respiratory infection. Hearing that, we all went into lockdown. That person was eventually tested for the corona virus. After almost a week the test came back negative; our self-quarantine ended. What a relief that was. But that event ushered our family fully into the bizarre new reality we're all learning to live with.

The Pandemic of 2020 has forced our family and people around the world to think, live, work and gather differently. It has disrupted the lives of hundreds of millions of people and ended the lives of tens of thousands. And that's just so far. I make my living working with business leaders and their teams. My professional life and the lives of my clients have been drastically altered. Many of the teams I work with are accustomed to being face-to-face to get work done. Most of them are comfortable with video meeting technology but feel most productive when they are together in a room. Other teams I work with live and work remotely most of the time, gathering physically a few times a year. For them this is less of a strain, but its impact is still significant.

Now and for the next several months (or longer) there is no chance any of these teams can physically convene even for the most important or sensitive work. Add to that high levels of anxiety around the disease, forced isolation, as well as the strains placed on infrastructure that makes desktop video possible and teams everywhere are reeling, looking for ways to cope.

Technology at the right place and time

Thank goodness for tech like Zoom, Microsoft Teams, Slack and others. Outside of work my family is using a video app for virtual cocktail parties and dinners. It's a hoot, and the mutual support helps. Workplace teams enjoy similar benefits from virtual togetherness. Via video conference they are getting things done. As importantly, they are offering empathy and encouragement to colleagues struggling with the separation and the strangeness of it all. The displays of caring and support are wonderful, creative and inspiring.

I hear from my clients, those fortunate enough to be working, that as they regain their composure and their teams settle into this new normal, they are managing to get good work done. I love hearing that but this is what has impressed me most: a few are already looking ahead, wondering how they can be more than just good. They intend, as one person told me, "To return to excellence before we return to the office."

But are we looking ahead far enough? Will those teams ever return to an office? Tectonic shifts are shaking the foundations of how teams operate. As we struggle to keep our feet under us, the aftershocks of the COVID-19 quake keep coming. Factories and offices are shuttered. Roads are empty and commercial aircraft have more crew than passengers. Commutes have been reduced to however long it takes to walk to your home office, whatever that may consist of. And, as the air clears over Beijing, Brussels and New York, countries and companies will seize this opportunity. They can save millions in travel expense and office leases; employees will spend more time at their desks being productive and less time in planes, trains and automobiles. All this while organizations earn valuable carbon credits and contribute to a better environment. Three months ago, collaborative technologies were viable options for teams working apart. Today, their use is prescribed; tomorrow, it will be preferred. This is the time to prepare for that. It's in that spirit, and to support the many teams striving to return to excellence regardless of where they may end up, that I have written this little book.

Lessons from Mars

I spent 17 years at Mars, Inc. I devoted several of those years to working with and researching high performing teams. During that stretch I gained a deep understanding of what teams, including ones working remotely, can do not just to survive but to thrive. I am not talking about conventional team building, ropes courses and the like. (If you have read my first book, *Lessons from Mars*: How One Global Company Cracked the Code on High Performance Collaboration and Teamwork, that will be no surprise.) Typical team building relies on increasing personal familiarity and generic relationship building. Those exercises can be fun, decrease stress and increase satisfaction temporarily but they do not lead to better collaboration. The strongest teams take a different approach. They develop bonds based on shared purpose and specific collaborative commitments that center them, hold them together even when apart. And, they do it in ways that improve their results and their relationships.

In *Lessons from Mars* I describe the Framework for High Performance Collaboration (HPC). I explain the research that led to the Framework and how the Framework is different from other team models. Sprinkled throughout *Lessons from Mars* I talk about teams conducting meetings and workshops virtually. Most of the stories though, involved face-to-face team interactions. Working virtually got far less attention. This book addresses that imbalance.

Finding ways for teams to stay centered, connected while being separated, has with striking and unsettling suddenness become more urgent and important than ever. This book applies

4

the proven principles and practices of HPC to virtual working. It's a user's guide with just enough background and context so that the HPC Framework makes sense. Most importantly it provides practical tools so that the many, many teams that now find themselves working apart can return to excellence before they return to the office or factory. I hope with all my heart that you find it useful.

Chapter 1

The High Performance Collaboration Framework

With Slack, MS Teams, Skype and all the other collaboration tools at our disposal it should be easy when working remotely to keep a sense of team unity and maintain the quality of work, right? Unfortunately, even in a world where we are constantly connected, motivating a remote team for long periods is a struggle. Even before the emergence of COVID-19, team leaders and members were complaining to me about what was lost when most of their connections were virtual. One VP of IT, a champion of virtual working, told me that no matter how excellent the technology, "It's just not the same. You lose that sense of immediacy; you miss those subtle cues of body language. Even tone of voice is affected."

He's right, of course. And, over time, the deficiencies of remote collaboration can eat away at a team's sense of connection and sense of team identity. I call this losing the team's center, losing touch with those things teams orient themselves around. When a team's center doesn't hold it's inevitable that the work will suffer. But it doesn't have to be like this. I have worked with teams that use the remarkable tech available to them AND manage to maintain a sense of centeredness that leads them to outstanding results.

So how can you keep your team connected and centered through your organization's work-from-home mandate? My study of teamwork and individual motivation provides some insights.

A different approach to teamwork

My research at Mars, Inc. was the basis for my book, *Lessons from Mars*: How One Global Company Cracked the Code on High Performance Collaboration and Teamwork. It started because we realized that conventional team building was not making a difference to how teams worked together to deliver results. When we dug into what was preventing teams from being more effective together, we made several surprising and important discoveries. Those discoveries shaped the Mars High Performance Collaboration (HPC) Framework, the novel approach to team effectiveness that I introduced in *Lessons from Mars* and have built this book around. What distinguishes HPC from other kinds of team building? The foundational insight from our research was a surprising paradox:

Team collaboration depends on individual motivation.

Most approaches to teamwork assume that the place to start when working on team effectiveness is relationships. There's no denying that collaboration has an important interpersonal aspect; as I've said it's one of the things that suffers when teams are forced to work apart from each other. But are our relationships the key to effective collaboration? Our research, which involved data from hundreds of teams, revealed that while relationships and the social aspects of teamwork matter, focusing on them as a precondition to more effective collaboration doesn't make a lasting difference to team performance.

Maslow's Hierarchy of Needs, an early theory of motivation, illustrates this flaw in the conventional thinking:

At work we tend to default to the bottom-of-the-hierarchy, self-oriented ways of getting work done. And why not? After all, we were hired as individuals and are paid, reviewed and promoted as individuals. Typical relationship-based team building ignores our lower-order, self-focused inclinations pushing us up the hierarchy to the relationship-oriented levels, whether we care to go there or not.

Our lower-order drives are powerful, though. Soon after the team building is over, those drives act like gravity pulling us back down towards things that feel important to us, the work we were hired to do and that puts bread on our tables. That response and that instinct are normal and not themselves bad things. In fact, some experts believe our inclination to get back to our own work is a major ingredient for success at work.

Another theory of motivation talks about this drive as the "need to achieve". It's one of three needs David McClelland identified as essential for success at work (the other two needs are affiliation and power.) This need to achieve, which is high in some people, moderate in some and lower in others, is something companies seek out. "Self-starter", action-oriented", "goal focused", are just a few of the terms you might see in a job posting that describe the need-to-achieve organizations so prize. It's no surprise, then, that Western-style companies are full of achievement-driven individuals whose achievement instincts during typical team building activities are ignored or actively discouraged.

That doesn't happen with the HPC Framework. It acknowledges this powerful individual drive, framing collaboration not as an attitude towards our teammates or a mindset but as a specific, tangible thing to be achieved. It's this foundation in individual motivation that sets HPC apart.

The six Practices of HPC form an integrated, action-oriented framework for teams that helps them unleash powerful collaboration. Each Practice has one or more tools associated with it. The tools are designed specifically to engage achievement-driven team members in work that will help them achieve even more via collaboration.

In the balance of this chapter I explain the Practices. In each subsequent chapter I provide one or more tools for each of the six Practices, each one designed for teams working virtually.

Overview

As I mentioned, the HPC Framework has six Practices. This overview defines each Practice and explains how the Framework functions as an integrated, dynamic whole.

The Practices of HPC

We depict the HPC Framework using the graphic below. It shows all six Practices and suggests the relationships and connections among them:

Why they are called "Practices"

The HPC Framework is not a set of stages a team passes through. Instead, it describes things teams focus on and do in order to become and remain high performing. Just as physicians or attorneys practice medicine or law every day, great teams continually practice the art and science of collaboration in order to be their best. Over time the Practices become good habits and the formal Framework fades into the background, becoming "just the way we do things around here".

The arrows in the graphic point to the left, right, and outwards from the center, conveying that each of the Practices interacts with those around it. It's those dynamic relationships that give the Framework its power.

A Guide to the Practices

Each Practice summary includes:

- A definition of what the Practice addresses
- The Core question it answers for the team and a few related questions
- Important links to other Practices
- Why the Practice works

The Practices of HPC

Inspire Purpose

Inspire Purpose addresses a team's collaborative *Why?* providing a sense of shared meaning that motivates team members to collaborate.

What it addresses: Clarifying the value, meaning, and importance of the group's collaborative efforts.

Core question: Why does this team exist beyond our obvious reporting or functional relationships?

Questions that support the Practice:

- Why do we exist as a collaborative group?
- How can we create unique value through our collaboration?

Why it works: Study after study has shown that, more than a paycheck or benefits, it's meaningful work that motivates people. Organizations have visions and missions. The real work of organizations, though, happens at the individual and team level. Inspire Purpose is a deeper dive into the personal 'why do I choose to be a member of this team'? This Practice clarifies the importance and meaning of a group's collaborative work through developing an inspiring purpose statement relevant to every individual on the team and what motivates them.

Key links to other practices:

- *Crystallize Intent* – The team's Purpose is the filter used for deciding which work requires collaboration and which doesn't.
- *Cultivate Collaboration* – Team Purpose is used to select behaviors required of team members to live fully into their shared aspirations.
- *Activate Ways of Working* – Teams use their purpose statement to assess the relevance of proposed meetings.

Crystallize Intent

Crystallize Intent focuses on crystallizing the *What* for the team, the work the team will do – or not do – together that supports their inspiring Why.

What it addresses: Creating and maintaining clarity about the specific projects and initiatives that require collaboration among team members, and those which don't require it.

Core question: What specific projects and initiatives require collaboration, and at what levels?

Questions that support the Practice:

- What work requires collaboration and what work does not?
- Who is assigned to each piece of work?

Why it works: When was the last time you and your team stopped and asked yourselves, "Of all the work we have, which projects or initiatives will benefit from collaboration and which won't?" And then, "Of all the work that *will* benefit from collaboration, what's the right level of collaboration—how many of us need to be involved?" If you have had these conversations, congratulations. You're in a productive minority. If not, this kind of clarity will connect individuals' drive to achieve with more intentional collaboration and effectiveness.

Key links to other Practices:

- *Inspire Purpose* – A team's purpose statement is the primary filter they use to decide which tasks and initiatives, if any, will be shared by the entire team.
- *Cultivate Collaboration* – During Crystallize Intent, team members specify which work requires collaboration and which team members need to be involved. These groupings then work together in Cultivate Collaboration to agree on how they will collaborate.
- *Activate Ways of Working* – The work that the team agrees to share in Crystallize Intent guides what goes on meeting agendas, a major topic in Activate Ways of Working. Teams also use the output of Crystallize Intent to agree which work requires shared decision making and which doesn't.

Cultivate Collaboration

Cultivate Collaboration focuses on fostering more intentional working relationships that support the team's *Why* and *What*.

What it addresses: Creating clear accountability for collaborative work. This Practice includes contracting for the expectations of collaborative behaviors between the leader and team members as well as between team members. It also addresses trust between team members.

Core Question: Who am I, who are you, and how will we work together most effectively?

Questions that support the Practice:

- What commitments will we make to each other about the work we'll share?
- What commitments will we make to our leader about how we will collaborate?
- How will we build strong relationships in service of our shared work and the team?

Why it works: When responsible team members see their names against specific tasks they have agreed to collaborate on, they respond with action. When they see their names paired not just with actions but also with the name of a teammate, their sense of responsibility extends to include their relationship with that collaborative partner. This natural response, accepting accountability for one's working relationships, is the heart of this Practice. Another part of this Practice involves leaders clarifying how they'll hold team members accountable for both the work *and* their collaborative behaviors. With new clarity and heightened accountability, the entire team can buckle down and figure out their collaboration needs and make specific commitments to each other.

Key links to other practices:

- *Crystallize Intent* – The decisions made in Crystallize Intent about which team members will be sharing which work with whom sets up the contracting conversations that are the core of Cultivate Collaboration.
- *Sustain & Renew* – Sustain & Renew is about on-going learning and improvement. It's the Practice that asks team members to check in with each other on how the collaborative agreements made in Cultivate Collaboration are working, what might need to change or improve.

Activate Ways-of-working

Activate Ways-of-Working focuses on establishing team processes linked to the team's purpose and shared work. Unlike Cultivate Collaboration, which focuses on behaviors and behavioral contracting, Activate Ways of Working deals with team-level processes.

What it addresses: Creating and maintaining a few simple team processes and norms for how the total team will operate in line with its purpose and collaborative commitments.

    Core question: How will we work efficiently and effectively together?

Questions that support the Practice:

- What meeting formats will we use for specific types of meetings?
- How will we operate most efficiently and effectively to deliver on our collaborative promises?

Why it works: Most team models include something about

team processes. What makes this approach different and more powerful is the way it links a team's purpose and collaborative agreements to their operational norms. Teams using HPC don't adopt generic "best practices". Instead, they craft a few custom routines around things like meetings and team communications tailored to *their* purpose and agreed collaborative work.

Key links to other practices:

- *Inspire Purpose* – The team's purpose statement is one filter teams use to ensure their meetings align with what matters most to them.
- *Crystallize Intent* – Crystallize Intent spells out which work the team shares, and therefore, is appropriate to include in meetings. This Practice also can provide guidance about what decisions should be shared and which can be left to individuals.

Sustain & Renew

Sustain & Renew engages teams in reflecting on and planning for how they will sustain and enhance or renew their team effectiveness and learning going forward.

What it addresses: Establishes a discipline of evaluating the effectiveness of agreed processes and updating where necessary. It is also about ongoing learning focused on how the team is or is not functioning. From this information, teams can create and maintain a team development and growth plan.

Core question: What must we attend to so that we can improve now and for the future?

Questions that support the Practice:

- What is going on within our team now and what do we

need to do next to take our collaboration to the next level?
- How will we keep learning and growing?

Why it works: High performance requires ongoing reflection, learning and growth. Many achievement focused team members are not innately reflective. This Practice makes learning a team routine, a good team habit to be developed and sustained. It establishes a rhythm of learning that team members come to expect, a rhythm that if broken feels like a lapse, a short-coming that achievement-driven people will seek to set right. Sustain & Renew makes on-going learning a goal to be striven for.

Key links to other practices:

- *All Practices* – Sustain & Renew invites teams to revisit and examine all the other Practices in the spirit of on-going learning and improvement.

Clarify Context

Clarify Context ensures teams understand the business and/or organizational context they are operating in. It helps them manage change and transition, to adapt their collaboration to suit changing circumstances. It resembles Sustain & Renew but focuses outward, on the team's working environment.

What it addresses: Clarifies how a team fits into the larger organization. It's activated only during periods of significant change or transition when a team should assess the conditions and circumstances they're working in. This enables the team to make smart, adaptive choices.

Core question: What is the bigger picture here and what does it mean for us?

Questions that support the Practice:

- What has changed in our environment and circumstances that we need to respond to?
- How do we need to change and adapt to what's going on around us?

Why it works: A business team's existence depends on the organization's needs. This Practice ensures that a team stays connected to the external organizational realities that created it and make it relevant.

Links to other practices:

All except Sustain & Renew – If the environment a team is working in shifts significantly – new strategy, new leader, new organization structure or the like – affected teams must review all the thinking they have done, from the value-add of their collaboration (Inspire Purpose) to which work requires collaboration (Crystallize Intent) to how they run their meetings (Activate Ways of Working) to ensure needed changes are made.

A few practical considerations

A sequence for working through the Practices

Most teams begin the HPC process with Inspire Purpose, since it is foundational to the other Practices. They then proceed clockwise through the framework to Activate Ways of Working and Sustain & Renew.

When to start somewhere else

There are times when working outside this sequence makes sense, especially for teams already using the HPC Framework. For example, a team may do a Sustain & Renew self-assessment and decide that their ways-of-working aren't supporting the shared work identified in Crystallize Intent. They would start working on Activate Ways-of-working to get things aligned. Or, perhaps a team is finding that relationships among certain collaborative partners are fraying. In that case, they would focus on Cultivate Collaboration.

The role of questions and dialog in HPC

Practicing HPC is not top-down or directive, something the team leader owns. While the manager or any other team member may guide the process, success with HPC relies on everyone in the team participating and having a stake.

Team dialog is fundamental to implementing and sustaining the Framework. To enable dialog, the practices of HPC are grounded in questions, as you probably noticed. Each Practice includes a core question and a few related ones that teams discuss, debate and eventually come to an agreement on.

Given this dependence on dialog, teams embarking on HPC need members capable of – or willing to become capable of – open, candid conversation and solid listening skills.

Don't worry if your team isn't there yet; many teams aren't. Using HPC, conducting the exercises in this book, can help your team get there. The tools offer a tested, potent means of practicing and developing foundational relationship skills that are essential not just at work but in all facets of life.

If you're a team leader and this is new to you, you may doubt your skills at fostering productive team dialog. Chapter 8 of this book offers thoughts on what it takes to lead a team through HPC including tips to foster open, candid conversation.

Next Steps

You now have a high-level picture of the HPC Framework as an integrated whole. You have the information you need to explore the tools for each of the Practices and put them to work to support your team on their HPC journey.

Chapter 2

Inspire Purpose

Part I: Practice Overview

If your team has relied on face-to-face interactions to sustain a sense of belonging and shared identity, these must be tough times. Lock-downs, shelter-in-place orders, and quarantines mean that you cannot, must not, be together in the same place at the same time.

You and the team will, at least for now, need to let go of your dependence on in-person interactions to center your team. Inspire Purpose provides a powerful, alternative way to strengthen the bonds among you in ways that will outlast needing to work remotely.

Teams that practice Inspire Purpose begin by creating clarity and understanding about the unique contribution of their collaboration, and how their work together will add value beyond their functional results. An effective and inspiring purpose statement is aspirational and connects personally with each team member, inspiring them to participate and contribute to the work of the team in meaningful ways.

What's involved

Developing an inspiring yet pragmatic team purpose statement and then applying it to the rest of the Practices and all your collaborative efforts.

The Power of the Practice

The goal of the HPC Framework is to leverage your team members' innate achievement drive. An achievement driven person is drawn to work that feels like it matters, that needs doing and that they can feel good about accomplishing. Such a person might ask about any task, whether it's collaborative or not, "Why is this important?" and, "Why do you need ME to do it?" A strong purpose statement clarifies *why* team collaboration is important and *why* each team member needs to be involved, making collaboration feel like just another thing to be achieved.

Part II: Tools and Techniques

Conducting a Team Purpose Conversation

Introduction

Developing a team's inspiring purpose statement is more art than science. Below is a conversation-based approach for developing your team's purpose that lends itself to remote teams.

NOTE: I am often asked to share examples of "good" purpose statements. There is no objective way to judge a purpose statement, what's good is what works for the team. For the curious, at the end of this chapter you will find a few examples of purpose statements that worked for the teams that developed them.

The "What-Who-How" Approach for Purpose Statement Development

This approach to purpose statement development was created by working backwards, beginning with a purpose statement that was proven to be effective. The structure suggested by that purpose statement has three elements, What, Who and How, that correspond to these three questions:

- What will our collaboration be in service of?
- Who will we be together?
- How will we play that role?

The process for distilling the elements of your team's inspiring purpose follows this "what, who, how" sequence. The final statement, however, is put together in the reverse order: "how, who, what".

The purpose statement that served as our model came from a team leading a pet food and products business. Here's how their statement maps to our structure:

- Their collaboration was in service of what larger ambition? Creating the future of the pet care industry.
- To support this ambition, they agreed they would act collectively as architects.
- They further agreed on how they would have to play this role choosing the adjective, courageously.

Their final statement read:

Together we are courageous architects of the future of pet care

Your statement may be longer or shorter or different in myriad other ways. The essential thing is to have thorough, thoughtful conversations, and to allow the statement to emerge from the group's interaction.

"Why," you may ask, "if a purpose statement acts as a team's collaborative 'Why', does your structure not include that very question?" Because, as any parent of young children can attest, "Why?" is a surprisingly tough question. It's open-ended and requires abstract thinking in service of getting to a concrete answer. That's tricky even with adults. You have probably heard of the root cause analysis tool called, "The Five Whys". Using it involves exactly what the name implies, asking, "Why," five times until you finally get to a problem's root cause. I've used the tool with groups and had to ask "Why," 7, 8 or 9 times to get close.

The What-Who-How approach uses "what" as a proxy for "why". Remember, the full question, is "What is our collaboration in service of?" That larger goal or ambition, the thing you are in service of is, in fact, the team's "Why?" Groups find the "what" question relatively easy to generate answers for. That's why we use it in our exercise.

Before you start the exercise:

- This process can take anywhere from 2 – 4 hours depending on the size of your team; small teams require less time. The timings we suggest are based on a team size of from 5 – 8.
- Assess the capabilities of your technology. This process relies on subgroups having a series of two – three conversations and then reconvening the larger group to debrief and discuss. Before you begin, determine if your meeting app allows for the creation of subgroups within the larger virtual meeting OR if you will have to have subgroups create separate smaller meetings for their conversations, and then return to the larger meeting. Either way works but it's important to know which approach you will use before beginning
- To enable the "What" conversation, you will need to Clarify Context for the team. Find and have ready any documents that could help explain how your team fits into the larger organization's (or function's) strategy, vision, mission, etc. This context is essential for ensuring your team's purpose is relevant to the broader organization. You may even want to run a Clarify Context session. The instructions for that are in chapter 7 of this book.
- If you have a team smaller than five people, modify the exercise so that you all work together on each step. If your team is larger than eight, modify the process accordingly, creating more subgroups as required.
- Subgroups of three people are optimal. Groups of four can work, but we recommend not exceeding four people per subgroup; larger groups slow down the discussions

making the process cumbersome. Groups of two can also work but are not ideal as the smaller number lessens diversity of thought.

The Steps

Before the workshop

1. Send an email summarizing what the team will be working on and why.
2. Send an invitation to the team for an initial 2-3 hour workshop.

During the workshop

3. Gather your team in your virtual space.
4. Briefly review the process based on your earlier email.

THE WHAT

5. Explain the team will first work on clarifying the "What" portion of the draft purpose statement.
6. Explain that subgroups of 2 – 4 will answer the question, "What is our total team's collaboration in service of?"
7. Share whatever information you have about your organization's or broader function's strategy, vision, mission or any other relevant strategic information.
8. Help shape their conversations by encouraging them to think beyond the obvious, i.e., making products or more money. Instead, they may be in service of a better future, more engaged employees, a healthier world, a more mutual business, etc.
9. Direct them to spend 20 minutes in their subgroups sharing ideas that answer the "What" question (see step

6, above) and to then narrow those ideas down to their preferred two to three ideas.

TIP: The more subgroups you have the smaller the number of preferred ideas you will want each group to bring back.

TIP: The selected ideas work best when expressed in short phrases of a few words, e.g., the future of pet care, healthier employees, etc.

10. Using whatever your technology will allow, break your group into subgroups
11. Reconvene the total group and allow each group to share its 2 – 3 phrases that clarify the "What".
12. Facilitate a conversation that might include merging ideas, building on ideas, etc. until the group agrees on one short phrase that captures the team's most compelling, "What".

THE HOW AND THE WHO

13. Explain that for the next two parts of the purpose statement, subgroups will work on one or the other of the parts, the Who or the How.
14. Determine who will be in which group.

Note: For larger teams, there may be two groups working on one or both parts of the statement.

15. Explain that the Who group will brainstorm about an inspiring role this team could play that supports the team's What, their collaborative ambition. Tell them to think in terms of archetypes such as entrepreneurs, architects, stewards, curators, ambassadors, champions, etc. Encourage them to use internet resources to broaden

the pool of possibilities.

16. Explain that the How group will generate ideas about how this team should play its role, using adjectives that they think would describe their collaboration at its best: courageous, inspiring, persistent, innovative, driven, etc. Encourage them to use internet resources to expand the pool of possibilities.

17. Tell the subgroups that volume helps. Encourage them to generate as many ideas as possible but to come back to the larger group with only their top three suggestions.

18. Send them off to their subgroups for approximately 20 minutes.

19. Reconvene the total group and ask the Who group to share its recommendations.

20. Begin the debrief by seeking additional ideas from those who were not in the group.

21. Then move the conversation towards agreement on one or two archetypal roles the team could play.

22. Repeat steps 19 – 21 for the How group, ending up with 2 – 3 adjectives that could describe this team at its collaborative best.

NEXT STEPS

21. Create a working group of not more than four members who, following this workshop, will craft and then propose two – three draft purpose statements based on the outputs of today's workshop: the suggested What phrases, the agreed upon Who archetypes and the short list of adjectives from the Who conversation.

22. Schedule a time for a meeting where the working group will present their two – three drafts.

After the workshop

23. During the meeting scheduled in step 22, facilitate a discussion leading to a single draft the entire team can get behind. Test it against the BeCAUSE framework, below.

24. Revisit your purpose statement in 4 – 8 weeks to test that it still feels relevant and inspiring. Adjust it as appropriate.

Note: I have had great success using pictures and photographs as part of this exercise. When we do the exercise in person, instead of having groups create lists of words, I give each breakout group a set of picture cards, like the Visual Explorer™ cards available from the Center for Creative Leadership. Using images tends to free people from the limitations of words and vocabulary, taking them into a more imaginative space. I tell them to spread out their deck on a table and, working silently, have each person select one or two pictures that they feel are relevant to their focus, e.g., the What, the How or the Who. Once every subgroup member has selected a card or two, they show their cards and then talk to each other about why they chose the card(s) they did. *When we do this virtually*, I instruct subgroups to use Google Photos or a similar online repository of pictures. They search for concepts they want to illustrate and then either download them or use screen capture to grab a couple of images which they put on a PowerPoint slide. They discuss their choices as a subgroup, and select a few to share with the larger group. From that point the process is the same as step 19 onward, above.

The BeCAUSE Checklist

Once the team has a solid draft, assess it using the BeCAUSE tool. Compare your statement to each of the BeCAUSE elements to see how strong it's likely to be.

Be: What and how will our team "be"?

It's about how you want to be with each other, and what you want the team to be to your people and to the business. It's not about functional goals, tasks, or outcomes.

C: CATCHY—sticky, clever, memorable.

The purpose statement should catch your attention, and the elements should stick with you because they are memorable.

A: ASPIRATIONAL—hopeful, appreciative, future-focused.

The purpose statement inspires the team to move forward with hope. It does not describe the current state but the future ways of being that the team wants to attain.

U: UNIQUE—original, differentiating, distinctive.

The purpose statement communicates the unique contribution of this team. The statement is an original creation unlike any other team's. It is not a replica from the level above but differentiates the team from others.

S: SHORT—concise, brief, crisp, simple.

The purpose statement should be easy to remember and share because it is brief and concise. Refine the statement to the simplest form while retaining all the attributes listed above. Team members should be able to remember and repeat it easily. Most teams print their statement so members can post it near their workspaces as a reminder.

E: EVERYDAY—useful, practical, consistent.

A purpose statement must be easy to understand and have practical everyday application. It provides direction for meeting agendas, directs decisions, and guides thinking about how the team works.

Examples of purpose statements:

There is no 'perfect' or 'right' purpose statement for a team. What is powerful and inspiring for one group may be relatively meaningless for another. What matters is what works and inspires you and your team.

- We are entrepreneurial stewards of the people and brands entrusted to us. (Leadership team of a small business unit considered a pipeline for future talent and developing brands)
- We inspire every marketer to unlock the growth potential of our brands. (A global team of marketing leaders, all of whom reported into separate geographies and businesses)
- We build a culture and leaders that believe in the innate potential of every employee to make a difference within and beyond the business. (A Learning and Development leadership team)
- We nurture meaningful relationships that drive Breakthrough Value Creation and Revolutionary Results. (A finance leadership team)

Chapter 3

Crystallize Intent

Part I: Practice Overview

Remote collaboration fails when it lacks focus. Imagine you ask me to join a half-day team meeting starting at 5:00 AM my time so that we can accommodate colleagues in Europe and Asia. Then imagine that the meeting is a review, a series of updates on projects and tasks covering *all* the work the team is doing, whether it involves me or not. I am going to get up early and skip my morning exercise routine to sit through hours of content that I have little-or-no interest in and nothing at stake for. Now imagine how this meeting is going to make me feel, its impact on my instinct for action and achievement. Scattershot approaches to meetings like the one just described kill team engagement and energy, especially when meetings are virtual.

The most effective teams, working remotely or in the same building, develop collaborative focus. They know where collaboration is essential to delivering results and they center their collaboration around it. They know because they take time to crystallize their shared intentions, to specify where collaboration will add value and where individual effort is the better choice.

Crystallize Intent invites you and your team to stop and ask yourselves, "Of all the work we have, which projects or initiatives will benefit from collaboration and which won't?" And then, "Of all the work that *will* benefit from collaboration, what's the right level of collaboration—how many of us need to be involved?" These simple questions are eye-opening and powerful for most teams because this is the first time they are asking them. Once they do, they can focus their collaborative efforts as never before.

What is more, because not all work requires collaboration the Practice is liberating for capable individuals who no longer need to worry that they aren't being "good team players" if a given task doesn't involve others.

What's involved

- The Radar Screen exercise for determining levels of team collaboration required on the various projects and initiatives owned by team members.
- Determining who is going to collaborate with whom on the projects where collaboration is required.
- Regular updates to the Radar Screen as work evolves over time.

The Power of the Practice

Teams typically rely on shared goals to unite and focus them, assuming better teamwork will result. Our research uncovered this paradox: shared goals tend to drive more individual effort, not more teamwork. A shared goal taps into the achievement drive, yes. But team members respond by doing their *own* work, what they know best, in order to help achieve the goal. Shared goals are necessary to define success and to measure a team's progress towards it. But it's shared *work* that drives collaboration. Crystallize Intent creates clarity around a team's shared work, their specific collaborative accountabilities. This clarity taps into their drive to achieve and connects it to collaboration. This connection is strengthened because team members also know their collaboration serves a clear, inspiring shared purpose.

Part II: Tools and Techniques

The Radar Screen exercise creates a graphical representation of a team's collaborative center. Teams use this tool to identify which work requires collaboration and which doesn't. It also asks teams to differentiate between collaborative work that requires full team involvement and that which is better done by subsets of the team. A Radar Screen conversation can be conducted either face-to-face or virtually, using desktop video with screen sharing. Below is the process for remote teams.

Conducting the Radar Screen Exercise with Remote Team Members

- Time required: 2 – 3 hours. Timing will depend on team size, number of tasks and the complexity of the team's working environment.
- Use Skype, Zoom or a similar desktop video application to conduct the process. Some pre-meeting work will be required, as described below.

Before the session

1. A few weeks before your Crystallize Intent workshop, describe to your team what you mean by, "Crystallize Intent", as explained earlier. You want them to understand the process and why it's important.
2. Ask each team member to send you via email, before the session, a list of the discreet projects and initiatives that they're responsible for. Each item they submit will include the names or initials of all team members who will be working on it. Their lists should *not* include general job responsibilities, e.g., "completing weekly run reports" or "doing expenses", but only discrete projects or initiatives.
3. Prepare your draft Radar Screen (see the image, below) ahead of time in PowerPoint® or a similar presentation software package.

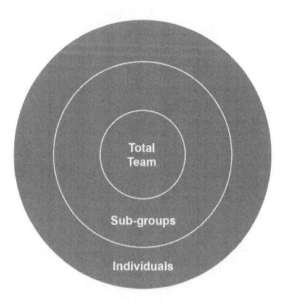

4. Populate your Radar Screen with the projects and initiatives that the team submitted.

- Place each of the items submitted by the team into an individual text box; one project or initiative per text box.
- Place each of the text boxes into the appropriate ring of the Radar Screen based on the number of people collaborating on each. Screen for duplicates as needed. Your virtual Radar Screen might look something like this:

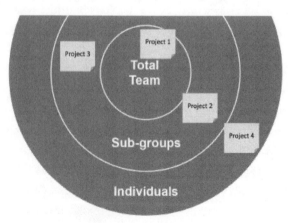

- Plan on sharing this draft Radar Screen during your virtual team discussion.

During the session

1. Begin by reminding the team how the process will work.
2. Share your draft Radar Screen via screen sharing so that it can be seen by all and modified in real time.
3. Start the discussion by having the team review the projects and initiatives at the center of the draft Radar Screen. Remind them that you only want projects in the center if they require the ongoing collaboration of the entire team. The goal is to end up with no more than three, maybe four, projects in the center by the end of your discussion. The projects and initiatives that are moved out of the center of the Radar Screen will be placed in either of the other two rings based on the discussion.

- Challenge the team to think critically about what requires full team collaboration as opposed to work that could be done just as effectively and more efficiently by either small groups or individuals.
- If, by the end of this discussion, there are more than three projects at the center of your draft Radar Screen, ask for suggestions on which ones should be moved to other rings of the Radar Screen.

4. Once you have got the Center of the Radar Screen to the smallest appropriate number of collaborative projects/ initiatives, conduct a similar discussion about the second ring of the Radar Screen.

- Remind the team that if a piece of work can be handled more efficiently and effectively by an individual, then it will be better placed in the outer ring.

5. Review the outer ring with the team to ensure that the projects there are indeed individual tasks.
6. After working through each of the three rings of the Radar Screen, ask one last time if there are any remaining concerns about placement of projects. Address any concerns through discussion.
7. Once the final version is agreed, take a moment to recognize yourselves for a job well done. Save a copy of the Radar Screen and plan on reviewing it again in three to six months and modifying it as circumstances change.

Chapter 4

Cultivate Collaboration

Part I: Practice Overview

Except for the most well-established team relationships, separation is likely to weaken interpersonal bonds among team members. Having a clear and compelling team purpose helps by creating a feeling of unity, of shared intent. Understanding the few, consequential pieces of shared work identified by the Radar Screen will further strengthen team identity. These two elements of HPC are powerful but can only do so much. Teams still need to proactively fortify relationships and promote effective collaborative behaviors to ensure the quality of their work together.

Most team effectiveness models take a generic, one-size-fits-all approach to relationships and team behaviors. Team members agree to "be good team players", and, "to build trust", with each other. Those are great intentions. Typically, that's all they are; vague intentions not clear or specific enough to guide behavior or to hold someone accountable for.

Cultivate Collaboration takes things a step – or two – farther. It focuses on fostering intentional, accountable working relationships and supporting behaviors anchored to specific tasks that align with the team's inspiring purpose.

What's involved

- Contracting for expectations of collaborative behaviors between the leader and team as well as among team members.
- Actively building trust among team members who are collaborating on specific projects/initiatives.

The Power of the Practice

The goal of our entire Framework is to make collaboration feel like just another thing to be achieved, to make teamwork connect with achievement-oriented team members. This Practice, Cultivate Collaboration, extends accountability beyond individuals to the quality and impact of collaboration. It ensures that collaboration and productive relationships are viewed as performance expectations. In doing this, the Practice connects with individuals' drive to achieve.

Part II: Tools and Techniques

Cultivate Collaboration begins with a two-way contracting process involving the team leader and team members. It's essential that these conversations be approached with care and a spirit of collegiality. It's not a matter of one person — the leader — foisting his or her will on a group or a group trying to get its way with the boss. (For more on how to lead HPC conversations generally, see Chapter 8.)

This exercise relies on fostering a sense of shared ownership among every person on the team, regardless of role. When I first went to Asia to run HPC sessions, I worried that deference to those in positions of authority, more common in Asian cultures than my own, would undermine this process. I got that wrong. Teams throughout Asia embraced this set of conversations frequently showing a greater willingness to engage with their leaders as partners than teams in the West.

The process involves crafting a set of agreements about what the leader and the team need from each other to make collaboration flourish. It involves negotiation, give-and-take, and the potential for disagreement. Therefore, conducting these conversations remotely requires patience, active listening and a blanket assumption that everyone involved has positive intentions.

Make sure you have access to video for these discussions and that everyone has their cameras turned on; these are not conversations that withstand distracted team members. If available, use gallery view so everyone is visible.

This process is comprised of five conversations, the final four of which can take place in a little over a half-day or be spread out over a week or two:

1. Set up the process – 15-to-20 minutes, done at least a week in advance of the other four conversations.
2. Team and leader develop their expectations and requests of each other – 45-to-60 minutes.
3. Team shares their expectations and requests of the manager and contracts for them. At the end of this conversation, the manager shares their expectations of the team. – 90 minutes.
4. Team processes the leader's expectations of them (shared with them at the end of the preceding step) – 60 minutes.
5. Team responds to the leader's expectations and requests, discussing and contracting for them – 60 minutes.

The process can be facilitated by the manager or any team member. I refer to whoever takes the facilitation role as, "the coordinator. The process flows as follows:

1. Setting up the process

A. At a dedicated meeting or as part of a longer meeting, the coordinator explains the steps, what the process accomplishes and how it will play out. If the coordinator is not the manager, ensure that the manager visibly commits to and endorses the process.
B. The coordinator explains that as a next step, team members, without the manager, will meet in order to prepare a list of their expectations of the manager.
C. The team leader agrees to do the same, to prepare a list of expectations for all team members collectively.

2. Team develops their expectations

A. The team gathers to develop their list of expectations of their manager. They will state their expectations as behaviors they need from the manager to support the collaborative purpose and shared work everyone has agreed to.

B. They put a finalized list of 8-to-10 behaviors onto one PowerPoint slide for use at the upcoming contracting session, conversation 3, below.

C. The team leader, working on their own, prepares a list of their expectations of the team. These expectations are stated as behaviors that the leader feels he or she needs from team members for collaboration to flourish in the team. The leader puts their expectations onto one PowerPoint slide for use at the end of conversation 3.

3. Team shares their expectations

A. The coordinator reminds the team of the purpose and outputs from this contracting session: a list of behaviors that the team and leader all agree the leader will commit to in support of the team.

B. Start with the team sharing their slide with expectations of the leader. For the moment, focus on questions for clarity and understanding, limiting discussion and debate. That comes later.

C. After the team has shared its list and the leader fully understands it, it is time to dig deeper. The leader works through the items, line by line and discusses

- What they agree with and why.
- What they are not comfortable signing up for.
- Ideas for how to modify suggestions so that every team member can commit to them.

D. This conversation continues until the team and leader either a) are comfortable with the requests as they are, b) agree to modifications or c) the team understands why their request(s) may not be included in the final behavioral contract.

E. Review the final list of behaviors for the leader. It's best if it's limited to five to seven easily remembered behavioral commitments. If necessary, pare the list down by merging similar or related requests.

F. The team leader ends the session by sharing the list of behaviors they developed for the team. Do not discuss these in depth at this point. Focus on being sure everyone is clear about what the leader presented. The discussion will come in conversations 4 and 5.

Note: As part of this step, the team leader must invite team members to be as candid as possible during conversations 4 and 5, below. The leader stresses their desire to learn from the team and their commitment to remain receptive to the constructive messages the team will deliver.

4. Team processes the leader's expectations

A. The team meets without the leader to discuss the list their leader shared at the end of the previous meeting.

Note: Meeting without the leader enables the candor essential to this process. Team members will want to encourage each other to speak their truth plainly, resisting the urge to "make nice", instead focusing on being clear and constructive.

B. They focus their discussion on developing a few kinds of responses:

• Expectations we can agree with as they are.

- Expectations that we mostly agree with but would suggest changes to.
- Expectations that we are struggling to understand or agree with.

C. The team prepares a slide or two summarizing their shared responses/questions.

5. Team responds to leader's expectations

A. The coordinator again reminds everyone what the intent and deliverables of this final conversation are.

B. The team begins by talking about where they agree with their manager's requests and why.

C. Next, they discuss suggested expectations that they think will be effective if they are modified somewhat. They offer specific suggestions for changes and discuss these with the leader.

D. The team shares those expectations that they are having the hardest time with. The goal here is to find common ground with the manager, not to make the manager wrong and the team right or the other way around.

E. This discussion continues until the team and the manager agree to the list of behaviors that will be expected of the team members. As with the manager's list, this list is best when it's limited to five to seven behaviors.

F. Debrief and discuss the final two lists, side-by-side. Check that both the manager and team can commit to their respective lists.

G. Led by the coordinator, validate the lists by checking them against the team's purpose statement and against the work at the center of the team's Radar Screen. Will these shared commitments support the collaborative intent of the team?

H. Print the final contracts and ask the entire team to sign them.

When the process is done, agree to how the team and leader will hold each other accountable for these behaviors. For example, many teams create scorecards that they review once a quarter. The team scores the leader and the leader scores the team.

Example of a Behavioral Contract

As team leader I commit to

- Assign tasks equitably.
- Support the team publicly.
- Hold us accountable for managing our own conflict directly with each other.
- Deflect non-priority requests from those outside the team.
- Be available for decisions and to resolve issues as required.

As team members we commit to

- Honor collaborative commitments or be clear when we can't.
- Keep the promises we make.
- Go directly to each other with conflict.
- Listen deeply for what's not being said, especially when in conflict.
- Challenge one another to exceed expectations.
- Communicate in advance of needs; limit fire-fighting.

Template for sub-group contracting

The second ring of the Radar Screen identified areas of collaboration for sub-groups within the team. The contracting among sub-groups is part of this Practice. Sub-groups use the template below for each project/initiative to be contracted (this template is designed for two people to contract. You can design a similar one for three or more team members) One template per one shared project/initiative.

What I will provide to you:	What I need from you:
•	•
•	•
•	•
•	•
Agreements for addressing conflict:	**How, and how often, we will connect:**
•	•
•	•
•	•
•	•

The entire team member contracting process can be done virtually using teleconference or desktop video. Use the template to propose your ideas for each shared project and your partners will do the same with their templates. Use a third copy of the template to record your final agreements.

Deepening relationships

As the Corona virus tightened its grip in the spring of 2020, several of my clients cancelled or postponed my work with them. Even ones for whom I had designed virtual sessions decided that relationship building done virtually was a bad idea; they insisted it could not be as effective as doing the work face-to-face.

Of course, virtual relationship building has limitations. Even with video, we're seeing in only two dimensions, missing more subtle visual cues. We're listening to audio that is often subpar. As one article I read years ago put it, working virtually where visual and auditory inputs are degraded decreases our "collaborative bandwidth".

Interacting on screen is suboptimal but it's far from useless. To the contrary, virtual relationship building can work and work well. This is especially true for teams who have already worked together to craft an inspiring purpose and who know why their collaboration is essential.

The virtual conversations I describe below are an opportunity to build trust and deepen relationships where it matters—between and among team members who share work. It is an approach that many of my client teams use, virtually and face-to-face.

When done face-to-face, the process takes 3 – 4 hours. Done virtually, this process typically requires 1) a full team meeting of 90 minutes-to-two hours, depending on team size, 2) a series of subgroup conversations that last anywhere from 15 – 30 minutes each, and 3) a final full team session to debrief the process.

The virtual subgroup conversations can happen the same day or be scheduled over the period of a week. I suggest you not go beyond a week because of the personal nature of the discussions and the disclosures involved; if not addressed promptly, the process loses immediacy and energy.

The Process

1. Ask each team member to prepare a slide or two with responses to these four points:

    - Three deeply held values that make me who I am.
    - Three things that energize me at work.
    - One thing that brings out the worst in me.
    - The legacy I dream of leaving.

2. Each team member shares his or her responses with the entire team. Encourage teammates to make notes as they listen.
3. Following each person's disclosure, facilitate conversation exploring how this person's responses might affect how they collaborate on team projects/initiatives shared by the entire team (those from the center of the Radar Screen). Invite questions from other team members who are curious to know more. Allow 10 – 15 minutes per person.
4. After all team members have presented, discuss how you will conduct the subgroup debriefs. Explain that each person will meet with their sub-groups (as identified in the Radar Screen) to discuss how the information they shared about

themselves in Step 2 could affect their shared work. Given the overlap of members across sub-groups this may require a few rounds for all sub-groups to complete the conversations.

5. While working in sub-groups be sure to refer to the sub-group contracts described above. This ensures that people's personalities and preferences are appropriately accounted for in your working agreements.

6. After all the subgroups have had their contracting conversations, convene a team meeting to discuss how things went, what the team learned and what adjustments they may need to make based on the conversations.

Chapter 5

Activate Ways-of-working

Part I: Practice Overview

The sudden need for teams to work apart from each other, sometimes for the first time, has made this Practice more important than ever. It's not news that virtual meetings are different from face-to-face meetings and are in many ways harder. Just the challenge of mastering the technology can consume hours, infuriating even people who thought they knew what they were doing. This chapter, though, isn't about how to use video meeting tech, how to mute yourself, turn your video off or invite new participants. It's about creating meeting agendas that are as relevant and compelling for team members as possible by applying the tenets of the HPC Framework.

Activate Ways-of-Working (AWOW) focuses on creating processes and routines centered around a team's inspiring purpose and shared commitments. In *Lessons from Mars* I provide tools for three ways of working: meetings, staying connected between meetings and decision making. In this short book my sole focus is meetings.

Teams that practice AWOW establish a cadence, a predictable flow of meetings with agendas centered around shared work that matters to all team members.

HPC users can, at first, confuse this Practice with Cultivate Collaboration since both deal with agreements about how team members will work together. As a reminder, AWOW is about team processes. Cultivate Collaboration focuses on accountable relationships and collaborative behaviors.

What's involved

- Designing meetings, a meeting cadence and meeting

agendas aligned with the team's purpose and shared work

The Power of the Practice

Most team models include something about team processes. What makes our approach different and more powerful is the way it links a team's purpose and collaborative agreements to their operational norms. Other approaches offer generic tips and tricks for better meetings. HPC-based meetings are more likely to engage team members because they deal only with topics and issues that every team member has agreed are important. This ability to engage participants is especially important for virtual meetings when attendees can easily become distracted and lose interest.

Part II: Tools and Techniques

Below are 1) an approach for figuring how often to meet and how long those meetings should be and 2) a method for building agendas around what are called "O^2" meeting deliverables.

Meeting Cadence: The Three Levers

Meetings can feel like a waste of time. Virtual meetings are even worse. Getting meetings right, therefore, is key to keeping your team vibrant and productive. A smart meeting schedule creates a balance among three factors:

- Meeting frequency
- Meeting length
- Agenda topics

Let's look at how the three interact to help create smarter meetings.

It's about time

Meeting frequency, meeting length, and even how one sets

up their agendas are all about wisely allocating meeting time. Finding the balance among these levers involves:

1. Figuring out how much time the team needs to spend together based on the work that was placed at the center of the Radar Screen.
2. Deciding how they prefer to divide that time up. That is, how often they need to meet to get their collaborative work done.
3. Agreeing to how long those meetings need to be.

How much meeting time, overall?

Meeting time is precious and costly, so budget it wisely. The higher the need for full team collaboration, the more shared work there is, the more time you're likely to devote to team meetings. Remember that not all collaborative work requires meetings. Sub-groups can handle parts of a project and bring them back to the larger group. A lot of collaborative working, even among the total team, can be done by sharing information and co-creating documents using file sharing and social networking applications like Microsoft Teams and Slack. Follow this rule of thumb: Allocate full team meetings only for those complex tasks and issues that will demonstrably benefit from it. Everything else can be done by individuals and small groups using collaborative technologies appropriately.

How often should we meet?

Frequency depends on the urgency and complexity of the work. If a project is on a short or urgent deadline, the team may need to meet frequently at least in the short term. Complexity can be a part of both short- and long-term projects. Complex projects, projects with multiple work streams and hand-offs within the team, benefit from high levels of connectivity among team members; meet more frequently in these cases. When urgency and complexity are combined in one project there is no substitute for using team meeting time as often as necessary to get the work done.

	LOW URGENCY HIGH	
HIGH COMPLEXITY **LOW**	Longer, less frequent meetings	Longer, more frequent meetings
	Shorter, less frequent meetings	Shorter, more frequent meetings

Collaboration technologies are also helpful for complex, urgent work, especially for remote teams working in different time zones. Between meetings, work can continue via file sharing, keeping momentum going until there's time to bring the team together again.

If the need isn't urgent or complex, meeting less frequently is fine. If a group is working together to create a long-range plan, and isn't bound by an immediate deadline, they can and should meet less frequently. There are likely other matters that are more pressing that will demand their time. Here again, collaborative technologies can be used to advance the work in-between actual meetings.

How long should our meetings be?

Especially when working virtually, short meetings are more engaging and effective. Studies vary when it comes to how long the average adult attention span is, but all of them talk in terms of minutes, not hours. Short meetings—an hour or less—are fine for straightforward topics and deliverables. Again, how long a meeting or meetings should be is a matter of complexity and urgency. More complex topics will often require longer periods of active collaboration than simple topics. Breaking up longer meetings on complex topics into a series of shorter ones can work; I like to limit virtual meetings to 60 minutes and vary the types of activities, switching among short presentations, small group discussions and large group conversation.

But, relying too much on short meetings can backfire. Interrupting productive debate or critical Q&A simply in the name of keeping a meeting short can compromise the quality of your meeting deliverables. Give the work and the meeting the time they deserve while staying mindful of participants' energy and engagement.

Though I separated them in the preceding explanations, meeting frequency and meeting length are two sides of the same coin. When it comes to setting meetings, you can think about frequency and length together with the help of the diagram above.

There are exceptions to this simple approach. Establishing a team's meeting rhythm is as much an art as a science. Take the time to consider the team's purpose, the nature of the work you share, and the overall environment you're working in. Apply this logic where it makes sense but be ready to flex.

Meeting agendas

Recurring team meetings

For regularly occurring team meetings, the work at the center of the Radar Screen forms the basis of your high-level agendas. If, for instance, your team has declared that it's working together on Projects Alpha and Beta, you'll put placeholders in your agendas for these projects. Of course, other items will make it onto your team's agendas. From time to time you will need to on-board new team members. There may be engagement activities you have planned. Occasionally, urgent matters will arise that require the team's attention. Any of these might need to be accommodated in a meeting agenda. But, when it comes to the regularly occurring work of team meetings, you turn to the Radar Screen first.

Your Radar Screen is a good start. When you begin to plan specific meetings, though, you must get more detailed.

The O^2 deliverable

Smart meetings have clearly stated deliverables and each deliverable is the result of active co-creation. We use the O^2 format for stating deliverables in the clearest way. Each O^2 deliverable is made up of two parts: the Objective and the Opportunity.

The Objective identifies in a general way what is being created or achieved. For example, we might be

- Co-creating a plan.
- Making a decision.
- Co-creating a solution.

The second O, Opportunity, refers to the specific benefit we'll get from the deliverable. We set this up as a "from–to" statement.

For example, maybe we need to decide (the objective) about moving FROM having three vendors TO having a single vendor (the opportunity). Another agenda topic might require an agreement (the objective) for moving FROM a variety of formats for submitting proposals TO one standard format for proposals (the opportunity.) The O^2 deliverable format forces greater clarity about what it is the team must accomplish. This focuses the team, helps them stay on track during the process, and helps you know when you have done what you set out to do.

Ad hoc meetings

Just because a piece of work isn't on your Radar Screen doesn't mean it might not require the attention of the team. Think about those urgent surprises that come up: an angry customer or a safety incident in a factory. Every so often teams have to call ad hoc meetings. These meetings benefit from the same thinking. Take time to frame a clear O^2 deliverable for even last-minute meetings.

Chapter 6

Sustain & Renew

Part I: Practice Overview

Sustain & Renew is the first of two Practices focused on team learning. Team learning involves a group seeking and gaining insight together in order to improve their ways of being and working together, whether they are remote or co-located, in service of higher performance.

To get individually motivated team members collaborating, HPC makes collaboration a thing to be achieved. The same thinking can apply to team learning. We move beyond the idea of learning as an occasionally useful by-product of our work, or learning-for-learning's sake, and frame team learning as an achievement objective.

The practice of contracting-for-learning includes making commitments to capture learning as a part of every project and every collaborative effort. The commitment to learn becomes part of team members' regular performance discussions. "What did you learn this year about how you collaborate?" becomes as common a question as, "What did you achieve this year?" The achievement motive is a mighty force. Without this transformation of learning into a recognizable achievement, learning, like collaboration, remains either a nice to do or an incidental outcome.

I had a conversation a few years ago with a General Manager at Mars renowned for her team leadership. Her people love working for her and she consistently gets strong business results. She told me that for the teams she has led, learning is non-negotiable. Every meeting ends with a review of what worked and what could have gone better. Every one-on-one with a team member includes a discussion about what they're learning and where they might be stuck. At the time we spoke, she managed a team spread out across the vast Asia-Pacific region. Even when working with her team virtually, the same rules applied. Not everyone who reports to her gets it at first. Eventually, though, most do. Those who don't take to it sooner or later self-select out. She told me, "At the beginning, when it comes to making the discipline of ongoing learning stick, you have to act as an unenlightened leader." In other words, to get teams used to treating learning as a performance expectation, you have to dig in your heels and be tough for a while. They can do it. They're just not used to it, not accustomed to being held accountable for it.

Sustain & Renew is inwardly focused learning, concerned with how the team is working or *not* working together. Clarify Context, the second Practice dealing with team learning, is outwardly focused on changes and events in the larger organization or world that the team may need to respond to. Both learning Practices deliver an important side benefit; through learning together, through high-stakes conversations that have important implications teams foster deeper connection, trust and psychological safety.

What's involved

- Assessing the team through regular, dedicated times of reflection and inquiry.
- Developing a plan of action based on the team assessment.

The Power of the Practice

High performance is not a destination, it's a journey. The vehicle enabling the journey is ongoing reflection and learning. In many Western-style companies, reflection is not encouraged or supported; action towards specific goals is the key to success. HPC recognizes this disparity and seeks to ensure that team learning becomes a specific, accountable goal for teams, one that speaks to achievement-driven individuals. What is more, and every bit as powerful as shared, achievement-driven learning, is the collective energy it fosters in teams.

True Team Spirit

What most people think of as building team spirit—creating a buzz, a positive sensation associated with team membership—produces nothing more than pleasant, short-lived feelings of connectivity. They're lovely feelings, but not lasting or change-producing.

There's another version of team spirit that's more valuable and more enduring. Teams using the HPC Framework begin by creating an almost tangible sense of team identity through their inspiring purpose and the clarity about the work they share. Then, guided by their shared purpose and work, they cultivate an environment of continuous learning and growth that leads to what I call "true team spirit".

Through Sustain & Renew teams foster a vitality that is sparked whenever they're together, virtually or physically. It nourishes them, draws them together when they have been working apart and keeps them feeling together when they must be apart. If you have ever experienced this buzz, you know what I'm talking about. I experienced it when I led the supposedly dysfunctional production team at the stock photo agency where I once worked. I had never worked with, let alone led, a group of photographers, production assistants and designers. For their part, they were only used to being told what to do by their erratic chief photographer who had limited managerial skills. For instance, they had never had a full-team meeting to prepare for a complex photo shoot. There were 10 of us, not including the chief photographer, and I thought preparatory meetings might be a good place to begin.

Our first team meeting was an awkward, confusing mess. It

made clear to all of us that we had a ton to figure out. How should I, with minimal professional photographic experience, work with these experts? How should they relate to me, a novice who was leading them but not technically their manager (that was the chief photographer's role)? As the weeks went on, we tussled, we worked through things and slowly found our footing. When outdoor shooting season arrived, we sweated together on location on hot summer days. But we did it together, learning as we went. Soon, we added debrief meetings after every shoot to identify what we had learned that we could apply at the next shoot.

During the year I was with them, the team taught me what it took to consistently produce top-notch commercial images that would sell; I showed them better ways to collaborate to get it done. We were making each other better every week. I'd never worked so hard, had so much fun or felt so bonded to a group. And, when it was time for me to move on, to a person they told me how thankful they were I had come along. I was just as grateful for having had them in my life.

True team spirit is that feeling you get around people, like the photo production team, who consistently bring out the best in you, whose energy and smarts you admire. You're drawn to these people because they kindle energy, intellect, and even vitality in you. This is team spirit well worth cultivating. It doesn't require motivational posters, paintball or trust falls; in fact, those things foster more cynicism than teamwork. Team spirit requires a focus on team learning and it can happen whether you are in the same office or oceans apart.

Part II: Tools and Techniques

The Team Learning Cycle

Team learning involves a group seeking and gaining insight together and then planning to adapt or improve based on their insights. It can be either inwardly focused or outward looking or some combination of the two. It involves examining team collaborative effectiveness, as well as the evolving environment a team is working in. There are three types of team learning, two of which I focus on in this chapter. The third is the subject of the next chapter. Here I'll share tools for:

- Task-related learning—focused on the work the team is doing together
- Team dynamics learning—focused on the way the team interacts and works together

The simple process we apply to either type of learning is a cycle of five phases that continually circles back on itself.

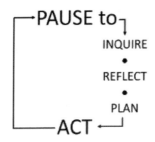

This cycle works for teams who are in the same building and for teams who only see each other on screens. I developed the cycle by observing high performing teams work through problems. Teams that did it best:

- Regularly set aside their busyness for a few hours, *pausing* with the sole objective of learning about how their work together was going.
- *Inquired,* collectively, into a few questions they posed for themselves.
- *Reflected* together and identified the insights gained from

their inquiry.

- Used those insights to *plan* changes to the way they were collaborating.
- Took *action* on their plans, made the necessary changes, and scheduled a follow-up in a few months to pause and check on their progress.

Team Dynamics Learning

When inquiring about team dynamics teams draw their questions for inquiry from the Framework. They ask things like:

- Is our purpose the right one? Is it still relevant?
- Is the shared work the right shared work? Do we need to add anything? Stop doing any of it?
- Is everyone living the behaviors we committed to in our Cultivate Collaboration work?
- Are our meetings well-aligned to our purpose and shared work? Do we need to adjust anything?

Remember: to tap into the achievement motive, team learning must be committed and accountable. The best teams, in times of disruption and in less extraordinary periods, begin the year by committing to a schedule of quarterly team dynamics learning sessions with ad hoc check-ins as needed. They also build into their standing agendas (see Chapter 5, Activate Ways-of-working) end-of-meeting debriefs to review what worked and what didn't. Today, as teams suddenly find themselves working remotely all the time, these post-meeting check-ins are especially valuable for learning to master the art and craft of remote collaboration.

The novel corona virus is an external event and, if we're being fussy, more a subject of discussion as part of the next Practice. There is no question, however, that this microscopic juggernaut has disrupted team dynamics. I suggest when the pandemic has passed teams should plan for a dedicated inquiry into how lessons they will have learned have strengthened and bonded them, and then go out somewhere to celebrate their growth and unity through tough times.

Task Learning

Task learning questions grow out of specific projects. The most effective teams use the cycle during and at the end of projects or initiatives and ask questions like:

- Have we organized the work optimally? Are the right people doing the right things?
- Are we off schedule? If so, what factors are contributing to the delay?
- Are we on track to deliver everything included in our original plan? Do we need to update anything?

More on Working Remotely

Sustain & Renew lends itself more than most of the Practices to teams working remotely. Inspire Purpose and Cultivate Collaboration, for instance, have specific deliverables; a purpose statement for one, behavioral contracts for the other. Sustain & Renew is open-ended. These are conversations of exploration and discovery with no predetermined outputs. Use the minimal structure of the learning cycle to give your discussions shape and direction, then let them unfold as the topic and circumstances require.

Given the relative simplicity of structuring learning conversations, almost every tool in your technology toolkit can be applied. For instance:

- Set up a brief, 5 – 10 minute, audio-only meeting to outline the learning process and explain what you want team members to come prepared to do. This simplicity gives team members the freedom to join via phone, tablet or computer from wherever they are, even if wi-fi bandwidth is limited.

- Share relevant documents beforehand using a shared drive. This gives team members a chance to digest important content before coming to the meeting and makes your meeting more efficient.
- Use video for Inquiry, Reflection and Planning; consider using virtual breakouts for doing deeper dives on specific topics. Smaller discussion groups can work through more in less time than a large group. Then they can share conclusions in summary form with the total team.
- Use an on-screen polling feature to get a sense of your team's level of agreement when needed. This technique is especially useful if the team is stuck on a decision and you want to break the logjam.
- If team members can't be present, record your conversations to be shared later with those who were absent.

Learning together is rewarding and energizing. It's also elemental. If you get nothing else right about this Framework but you figure out how to make team learning accountable and a regular discipline, everything else will fall into place. If your purpose isn't clear or useful, Sustain & Renew will surface that and you can address it. If your Radar Screen has missed the mark, do a mini Sustain & Renew session and you will get it sorted. If team members aren't living up to their commitments, pause, inquire, etc. and you will, with persistence, get back on track. In fact, you could say that Sustain & Renew with team learning at its core is the uber-competency for high performing teams.

Chapter 7

Clarify Context

Part I: Practice Overview

Max DePree in his book *Leadership Is an Art* says, "The first job of a leader is to define reality." Teams have the same responsibility; Clarify Context is how teams makes sense and meaning of the reality they operate within.

Business teams are initially created in response to organizations' needs; something needs to be done so a group is created to do it. Things change, though. The new reality of global pandemic has forced teams everywhere to take stock and adapt and to do so with stunning speed. One New York City-based financial services leadership team had to figure out in a matter of days how, with no interruption to their business, to move all operations out of Manhattan into less densely populated suburban areas. Less than five days after those decisions were made, after people, desks and technology had been relocated, every member of every team was told they would now be working from home. Another blazingly fast need to adapt but one they were ready for. As part of their initial "pause and inquire", they anticipated this second move and laid plans for it. As I write this, the leadership team is still responding but now to the impact of the pandemic on their clients, all of whom have been similarly affected. It doesn't stop. So, their need to learn at an unprecedented pace continues. The need for a discipline of on-going learning has never been more important.

This Practice gives teams tools to remain connected to evolving and/or rapidly changing organizational and global realities, allowing them to stay relevant and, in some cases, to survive. It asks groups to assess the meaning, impact and implications of changed circumstances they're working in. It enables them to make smart, adaptive choices about their collaboration.

Two other important points:

- Like Sustain & Renew this Practice is about the team learning together, specifically what I call Strategic Learning. Clarify Context differs in that it focuses outward, on the team's working environment instead of on the team itself.
- Because Clarify Context addresses a team's essential organizational reason for being, after applying it teams usually revisit some – or all – of the Framework. For example, if a change in your organization's structure results in your team being restructured, return to the Framework beginning with Inspire Purpose in order to re-center your team around its new role, purpose and shared work.

The Power of the Practice

This Practice clarifies for team members broader organizational challenges and opportunities that will affect them. It spotlights the importance and meaning of changes for the team. It asks team members to connect those changes directly to their work, whether that work is individual or shared. The added clarity and specificity tap into and ignite the power of the achievement drive.

What's involved

This Practice involves structuring inquiry conversations leading to insight and action using a tool I introduced in Chapter 6, the Five Actions of team learning. To help frame the changes and the conversations about them, we created five general categories of change, each with a set of questions to guide your inquiry. I list the categories and questions later in this chapter.

Part II: Tools and Techniques

Learning about context

Clarify Context is a big deal; you only invoke it when facing major changes or disruptions such as the corona virus epidemic now engulfing our world. The process is straight forward and simple to execute using collaboration technologies, but it can require more effort and energy than the inwardly focused conversations in Sustain & Renew.

It begins with the Five Actions adapted for outward focus. Here is what that looks like:

Pause: Clarify Context, because it's a response to big changes, can become involved. You will likely need more time to pause to allow teams to inquire deeply into potentially complex circumstances. In our age of pandemic, with multiple, rapid changes buffeting us, pausing feels like precisely the wrong thing to do. It's never been so essential. Teams are adapting how they learn together, finding ways to create space even when it feels like there is none. Many of these pauses are happening outside so-called "normal business hours". Daily, early morning team check-ins of not more than 30 minutes to assess and process the latest news. After-dinner (at least in the US) convenings of under an hour to evaluate progress and prepare for the next day. Longer weekend sessions to probe more thoroughly. I'm not suggesting teams do all of these. These are just a few ways teams I work with have modified their usual practices in response to the crisis of the moment.

Inquire: No matter what triggered the work on Clarify Context, regardless of its breadth or complexity, it's the team's inquiry into the meaning and impact of the change that is most important. Use whatever pauses your team has created for itself to study the situation together. If the situation is urgent or complex it may mean virtual meetings will run longer than I recommend in Chapter 5; inquire, anyway. Meet more often if needed. Practice Inquiry at the pace of the change that confronts you. Use the questions below or frame new provocative questions that will get people thinking and broadening their understanding.

Reflect: After digging deep into the questions you've posed, begin to make sense of it all. Look for connections and themes. Ask "How might these things be related," and, "What might these links be telling us about how to respond?" Keep asking until you feel you have landed on genuine insight. Talk about the "what", the implications for your work together. Don't settle for the easy answers early on, though in the end they may be what you return to; when pace is so important, so is honoring intuitions born of even modest reflection.

Plan: Address the "so what" of it all. What will this team do about what it has discovered? How, specifically should you move ahead? When? Who should do what and with whom? Include the Five Actions of learning as part of your plans to be sure you pause to gauge how things are working and adjust as needed.

Act: Put your insights and plans to work. If the change was significant with far-reaching implications, you may want to phase your responses. As we used to say at IBM when I worked there, don't try to "boil the ocean" but take things one step at a time. Again, be prepared to pause while in action, especially if responding to a crisis, to evaluate your adaptations and adjust them as needed.

Conversation Questions

There's a long list of possible events that a high performing, and therefore adaptive, team might need to respond to, to stay relevant. And, since we don't know what we don't know, that long list has to be incomplete. Trying to bring some helpful order to this, my colleagues at Mars and I originally identified four major categories of events that teams frequently need to pay attention to. They were:

- Changes in leadership.
- Changes in organization structure.
- Changes in strategy.
- Changes in team membership.

But, oh, how times change. Since the publication of *Lessons from Mars*, I have had to add another category: systemic change. The Pandemic is the perfect example of systemic change. It's change that changes everything; it affects not only the organization or its strategy but the entire system the organization is part of: supply chains, customers, financial markets, public infrastructure and so on. The events of September 11, 2001 created similar kinds of systemic changes in our personal and working lives. How arrogant of us when first devising our list of four types of change to think that something as far-reaching and broadly disruptive as 9/11 would not happen again in our lifetimes. We keep learning and now there are five categories of questions.

Below, organized by the five categories, are questions that are useful when facing each type of change. Decide which kind of change you are confronting and refer to that section.

This isn't an exhaustive list, just a starting point. Since life keeps showing us how amazingly unpredictable it can be, be prepared to build on and depart from the five categories. Also, these categories of questions can be combined and recombined to address a host of possible circumstances. I share thoughts on how to do that after the final set of questions.

Choose your category and questions and plan to hold a team meeting – or meetings – to explore them using the Five Actions.

Leadership change:

- As the new leader, what excites or worries me about this opportunity?
- What skills or capabilities do I need or need to develop in order to be successful in this role?
- What do I need to know about this role and this team that will help me to succeed?
- As members of the team, what do we want our new leader to know about us as a team and about our HPC journey so far?
- What are we most worried about as we make this transition?
- What is most exciting to us?

Organization structure change:

- What is this team's function in the new organization, broadly?
- Has it changed?
- Have our internal customers or stakeholders changed?
- Is our team set up appropriately to account for the changes in the organization? If not, what needs to change?
- How should our ways-of-working change to deliver value to the business?

Strategy change:

- What is the shift that has taken place in our organization?
- What do key customers think about what is going on in our organization?
- What are the goals, challenges and operational constraints that our organization is facing now and how have they changed?

- What does the organization want our team to achieve?
- How do we fit in?

Team membership change:

- How will we effectively on-board our new members and integrate them into our team?
- If new members are joining, what are their strengths and development needs?
- What is our team's working style and what are its implications for new members?
- Do we have the right capabilities on the team to deliver what the organization expects of us?
- What is each team member's level of readiness and willingness?

Systemic change

- How would we describe this event/change in one sentence, what is its essence?
- Just how disruptive is this event/change?
- How is this event/change likely to affect our organization?
- How might broader changes in our world and organization affect our team?
- What should our team be most concerned about as a result of this?
- What opportunities might there be as a result of this?

Creating hybrid sets of questions

Let's say your team has just been created and you want to do a Team Start-up Session. Treat it as a hybrid of three categories: organization structure change, team leadership change, and team membership change. Then structure your inquiry and reflection accordingly. Below are some recommended questions, altered slightly, and their categories. Use this as-is or as a starting point to create a list suited to your new team:

Organization structure change:

- What is this team's function in the new organization, broadly?

Leadership change:

- As the leader, what excites or worries me about this opportunity?
- As the leader, what skills or capabilities do I need or need to develop in order to be successful?
- As the new leader, what do I need to know about this role and this team that will help me to succeed?

Team membership change:

- How will we effectively on-board members and integrate them into our team?
- What are the strengths and development needs of team members?
- What is each team member's level of readiness and willingness?

An Example

The Mars global snack food business that includes brands like M&Ms, Wrigley gum and Starburst announced a strategy change last year. A new organization structure was readied for implementation in early 2020, one that included a redistribution of talent across R&D and Marketing. Just as the pandemic was accelerating, I was asked to work with a new team comprised of members coming from both functions. The new team would be reporting into the VP of Innovation, a new function that was mostly marketing-focused. They asked me to help them assess then address the implications of these changes for their team and to do it remotely.

The breadth of the changes meant the team and I would be answering questions from four of the five areas: strategy, organization, leadership and team member changes. There was another element that required attention, one that is common when big change hits. One of the members of this team had been expecting to get a senior role in the new organization. That didn't happen and she was carrying the baggage of that disappointment into our work together. Others resented being moved out of R&D, a function they were proud to serve, and into Marketing. There were other different but equally strong reactions to the disruption caused by the new strategy and structure; powerful feelings are a major part of any significant change. So, I had to account for this emotional reality in the upcoming Clarify Context work.

I designed a series of four, two hour video conference workshops that were preceded by a series of team member telephone interviews. In the interviews, I asked about what the changes meant to each person and how they were feeling about them. I prepared a summary of these discussions that I shared during our first video session together.

Session 1 – Getting connected: This would be this team's first gathering of any kind. Rather than jump directly into Clarify Context discussions, this was a chance to connect as people and to share their feelings about the changes. I facilitated a series of introductory exercises and then a debrief of the interview summary where emotions flowed freely. Coming out of these discussions I framed the next three Clarify Context discussions.

Session 2 – Addressing strategy and organization questions: These included, "What does the strategy have to say about our team's role specifically?" Related questions included, "What will be expected of us by other functions?" and "What resources/ budget will we have?"

Session 3 – Addressing leadership questions: These included "Who is our new leader, what is her professional and personal background; "What is her management style?" "What are her expectations for this team?"

Session 4 – Addressing team membership questions: This was a hybrid team with members from different functions. We posed and answered questions that accounted for this, such as, "What are each of our backgrounds, professionally and technically?"; "What skills, abilities and knowledge do we bring and how will they support the strategy?" and "What does each of us need to learn in order to play their role in this new team?"

The four workshops took place over two weeks. Even with clear questions for each of the four agendas, some of the discussion crossed boundaries; Session 1 conversations tipped over into questions from sessions 3 and 4. Session 2 got emotional as team members discussed how the restructure felt to them and it ran long. No matter. They got what they needed. By the end of Session 4 they were on the same page strategically; they had a shared sense of what they had just come through separately and where they needed to go together.

Using video was admittedly harder than if we had had the luxury of being physically with each other. Still, as we proceeded through the four sessions, we all got better at being present with each other virtually. People settled in and by session 4 you could feel a greater ease even when discussing more difficult subjects.

Coming out of the last session, the team agreed to embark on working through the other HPC Practices, starting with developing their collaborative purpose. That workshop is still being planned. Based on all you now know about the HPC Framework, it's probably clear that the team could not have a meaningful purpose discussion without first having done Clarify Context. This is a great example of the integrated nature of the Framework I talk about in Chapter 1 and how using it holistically is necessary to get its full benefits.

There are countless other circumstances where you could apply this questions-based, hybrid approach. The same logic will apply across most of them. Use my list-of-lists as a starting point and be creative when facing whatever may come your way.

I can't, I don't want to, imagine a set of circumstances where teams learning together will be more necessary than now. I hope we never see such times. For now, though, learning together is indispensable for teams, groups, communities, even nations. I hope you will use these ideas and tools to aid learning, living and eventually growth at all levels.

Chapter 8

Leading High Performance Collaboration

The tools and techniques in this book have helped hundreds of teams and tens-of-thousands of team members to feel and be successful. The tools alone don't do the trick. If you lead a team, how you use the tools is as important – if not more important – than the tools themselves.

HPC arose out of and in many ways reflects the Mars, Inc culture. To lead teams using HPC it helps to know something about that culture and how it shows up in the Framework. As I describe it in *Lessons from Mars* the Mars culture is deeply egalitarian. The spirit of egalitarianism pertains regardless of a person's title or where in the world you find them. Everyone from the President at global headquarters in McLean, VA to the hourly workers in factories from Hackettstown, NJ to Huairou, China is called an Associate. "Associate" is more than a trendy label HR came up with to make employees feel good. It represents a decades-old commitment to ensuring that everyone working at Mars, no matter where they are, sees him or herself as a valued and essential part of the company achieving its vision and goals.

> ...Each associate can expect to be respected, supported and valued as an individual, to be treated fairly and equitably, to be rewarded for their performance, and to have opportunities to grow and develop. This is a relationship of mutual trust, dignity and respect...which values people as individuals and allows their great talents to be released.

We hard-wired this commitment to respect, mutual trust and individual talent into the HPC framework. Every Practice-based conversation is built around the involvement of all team members regardless of title or role. Team leaders and team members work together with different but complimentary skills and responsibilities to bring HPC to life.

This way of managing and leading works at Mars and at other successful companies. Not all organizations and their leaders operate this way. But, if your company isn't like Mars, don't assume HPC won't work for you and your team. I've seen and heard about HPC working in all kinds of organizations, large and small, for-profit and not-for-profit in places around the globe. It's all about how you lead it.

One definition of a strong team leader is that they provide a better experience for their team than they themselves experience with *their* boss. Other studies say that as much as 75% of improvements in team engagement scores are attributable to the team leader. As a team leader, you have tremendous influence with those who report to you. If you are ready to use HPC, I have some ideas for you about how to lead your team through it regardless of where you live or work.

The Engaging Behaviors of HPC Leadership

People have been studying business leadership for over a hundred years and opinions abound about what makes a great leader. Despite the multitude of theories, most modern ideas of leadership share a focus on making work engaging and fulfilling for people. This is because there's abundant data suggesting that more engaged people produce better business performance.

Here's a partial list, based on research, of what leaders and managers do to drive high engagement:

- Give employees clarity about what needs to be done *and* the accountability for doing it.
- Provide the tools and processes they need to do their work.
- Foster the feeling that their opinions matter.

- Give people the freedom to decide the best way to do the work.
- Ensure they have opportunities to learn and grow through their work.

There's little news here. But, do you notice the parallels with how HPC is designed? For instance:

- HPC is grounded in *clarity* and *accountability*.
- The Framework gives team members *tools* and *processes* to enhance their collaboration.
- Every exercise in every Practice asks for and honors *team members' opinions*.
- HPC relies on *team members deciding* how they want to work together.
- HPC challenges teams to keep *growing* as a team and as individuals.

What this means for you, as a leader of HPC may be obvious, but here are a few thoughts:

1) Be Clear: Be clearer than you think you need to be about why your team's collaboration matters to the larger organization. Help them reach clarity about their team purpose and the work that will deliver on it. Be clear with them about their accountability for productive collaboration with teammates.

2) Provide tools and processes: Share this book and the Framework with your entire team. Show them the tools, explaining how they work.

3) Encourage participation and candor: HPC depends on team members choosing to participate and to have their voices heard. Role model curiosity, asking open-ended questions, and listening deeply. Affirm team member contributions and recognize when the team engages in productive debate.

4) Let the team decide: Invite the team into the HPC process early and let them shape how the team approaches the Practices, the tools and techniques.

5) Foster an atmosphere of learning: Create and hold space for team members to play with ideas, to test concepts, to try things without worrying about what you or others will think of them. When things don't work out, frame it as a learning opportunity and guide the team to deriving the lessons.

Some of these things may come naturally to you. Others will require you to stretch into uncomfortable areas. This is especially true if you are more accustomed to "leading from the front".

Your Leadership Stance

You may have heard about the three leadership stances: leading from the front, leading from the middle and leading from behind. All three are useful, depending on circumstances. As I suggested in Chapter 1, the Framework won't work if you insist on leading from the front, using a top down, directive style of leadership. You can't mandate powerful, accountable collaboration and the HPC framework won't work if you try.

Leading from the middle is essential to HPC; jump in and work with the team on the Practices while providing necessary guidance and coaching. Ultimately, if you get it right, you may end up leading from behind, allowing the team to chart the way forward, with you providing perspective, occasional support and championing their efforts.

In these days of volatility and uncertainty, of pandemic and isolation, the truth about how much we can control is laid bare. Both leading from the middle and from behind require letting go of control and cherished, if outdated, notions of leadership. This might be unsettling. But it's also liberating, freeing us from the million-and-one details we once felt we needed to manage. As the five items in the list above suggest, HPC works best when you cede control to your team over how HPC gets done. Use your authority not to direct but to role model openness and a willingness to try things even if they aren't perfect. Foster an environment within which the team can feel successful and succeed, learn and grow. Lead your team in ways that honor them for who they are and what motivates them, that tap into their innate strengths and sources of energy.

Our present predicament is unsettling in so many ways. It's also rich with possibility. It offers a chance to try things, test ideas, and learn new skills. It's also a time to show our organizations a new, fit-for-the-future practice of teamwork. HPC gives you a platform to do all this. Make a start and invite your team into the process. They will respond with engagement, commitment and better results. You may find unexpected sources of inspiration and fulfillment as you watch them flourish. Stay with it, master the Practices, and, importantly, shine a light on your successes. With your team, become a beacon lighting the way for your organization to embrace a new way to unleash the power of high performance collaboration.

Appendix: Virtual Meeting Tips

This list was created together with Tim Ward, co-author of the companion volume, Resilience: *Virtually Speaking –* Communicating when you Can't Meet Face to Face *(Changemakers Books, 2020)*

Activate the Agenda

- Keep virtual meetings to under one hour. After that, attention will flag. If you have more ground to cover, EITHER build in a break every hour OR hold more frequent, shorter meetings.
- Focus on topics that involve co-creation and decision making to drive involvement and engagement.
- Invite only people who will have an active role to play throughout the meeting.
- Limit info sharing in meetings; send short, digestible pre-reading that is relevant to the work you will do in the meeting.
- Use every technical tool you have that makes sense: polling, instant surveys, breakout groups, virtual whiteboards, etc.
- Plan to vary meeting approaches every 10 – 15 minutes: e.g., from presentation to gathering input via chat to polling to breakouts, etc.
- Minimize PowerPoint. Since the best meetings are about co-creation, avoid lengthy, info-sharing slide decks. Instead use only enough slides to frame the tasks the group is working on.

Tame the Technical

- Know your app, what it can and can't do, e.g., screen sharing, polling, chat, breakouts, etc.

- Test. Do dry runs a day or so before to ensure hardware and software work as planned. If using special features like polling or white boarding, test the features and be sure you can explain how to use them.
- Give guidelines to participants for setting up their virtual meeting seat: types of headphones, camera, managing noise, etc.
- Encourage all participants to test their hardware before the meeting.
- Start meeting 15 minutes early to ensure everything is working and ready.
- Have a plan B: if doing video, be sure to share a telephone number for any who need to call in. Send any slides to all participants in case they end up on the phone.

Show Your Best Self

- Face a light source (a window is best) and encourage participants to do the same. Seeing everyone's faces enhances communications by making expressions visible. Don't sit with your back to windows or bright lights as backlight makes faces dark.
- Bring your camera to eye level (e.g., place your laptop on a small box or stand); avoid looking down into your computer as if you were typing, forcing others to look up at your chin.
- Frame yourself with your head towards the top of the screen and ask participants to do the same.

Integrate & Involve

- Ensure everyone has video on (unless technical limitations prohibit it).
- In smaller meetings (eight people or fewer), get every

voice in the room early with a brief introductory exercise (e.g., one minute per person). For larger meetings, consider briefly introducing everyone yourself.

- If this is a regular team meeting, introductions are not necessary. Instead, start with a brief, relevant check in. For example, each person could say what for them is the top priority of the meeting.
- Share ground rules, like, "Cameras on," and "No multitasking." (The best way to limit multi-tasking is with a tight, highly involving agenda).
- Call on individuals as needed to keep the meeting moving and energy flowing.
- Write out names of participants for yourself if not all are visible on screen. This eases the process of calling on individuals when needed.
- Keep the pace crisp. Stick to your agenda and check occasionally that you aren't rushing past concerns or questions.
- Use breakouts early and often, especially for addressing subsets of complex tasks (for example, see Chapter 2, Inspire Purpose). Three – four people is ideal for subgroups. Larger groups tend to take longer without much added benefit.
- Always have subgroups report their findings/ recommendations to the larger group, allowing for questions and discussion.

Learn the Lessons

- Set aside the last 5-10 minutes to debrief the meeting: "What worked" and "What I wish had been different".
- Keep looking for latest tips on virtual meetings and experiment with them.

Author Biography

Carlos Valdes-Dapena (MFA, MSOD) is the founder of Corporate Collaboration Resources, LLC, an organization and group effectiveness consulting firm. He is a speaker and the author of the book, *Lessons from Mars*: How One Global Company Cracked the Code on High Performance Collaboration and Teamwork. Carlos developed his expertise in collaboration at the highest organization levels. For 17 years he was an internal consultant at Mars, Inc. and was involved with brands like M&Ms, Snickers, Uncle Bens Rice and Wrigley's gum. Before Mars, he spent three years at IBM as an executive coach and consultant to the top 35 global leaders at IBM including a number of CEO Lou Gerstner's direct reports. Carlos's consulting career began in 1993 when he was hired by DDI, a global talent development consulting firm, as a leadership and performance management consultant. At DDI, his client list included AT&T, Pfizer, General Motors, Lockheed Martin. He is the parent of two grown daughters and grandfather of two.

Previous Titles

Carlos is also the author of *Lessons from Mars*: How One Global Company Cracked the Code on High Performance Collaboration and Teamwork. *Lessons from Mars* challenges the prevailing orthodoxy of corporate team building and offers an alternative framework, along with a set of tools and techniques. Based on his 20+ years of experience working with teams, and six years of research specifically on teams at Mars, Inc. the book offers a unique view into this closely-held private company and how it has unlocked the power of collaboration.

What experts have said about *Lessons from Mars*

There are over 14 million results on Google when you search 'HIGH PERFORMANCE TEAMS BOOKS'—so what's great about this one? Carlos has accumulated a wealth of 'inside knowledge' on what makes the enigmatic Mars business tick. He's extracted the DNA of high performance and its impact, which we at Leading Edge have used as a guiding compass when developing collaboration with global Mars teams over the last 3 years. Ultimately, he's created a compelling story for modern business leaders and anyone interested in decoding high performance.

Patrick Marr, *Managing Director, Leading Edge Consulting*

Carlos's conversational style, his humor and pragmatism keep you reading; he combines theory and practice with elegance and thoughtfulness. His work drives home the point that the key to effective teams at any level is a clarity of purpose, role and expectations which support greater intentionality, clarity and discipline leading to effective outcomes.

Harris Ginsburg, *former VP, Executive Leadership and Talent Development, Pfizer, Inc.*

There may be no "I" in team, but there is in "informative", "interesting", "innovative", and "insightful" — all apt descriptions of *Lessons from Mars*. Building on his nearly 30 years in the field, Carlos Valdes-Dapena takes a hard look at what passes for team building in the corporate world and finds it wanting. But this is more than a critique of conventional wisdom by a consultant peddling his own approach. After thoroughly dissecting the ineffective way most companies spend their money on team effectiveness, this book offers a cogent, research-based alternative that can be used by anyone managing groups of people. It turns out that while women are from Venus, valuable lessons in corporate management are from Mars, Inc.

Roy Sekoff, *Founding Editor, The Huffington Post*

Note to readers

Thanks for buying *Virtual Teams*: Holding the Centre When Your Team Can't Meet Face-to-face. I hope you enjoyed reading it. More importantly, I hope you put some of these tools to work for your team. If you have a few moments, I would appreciate your writing a review of *Holding the Centre* at your favorite online book seller.

If you've had a chance to use any of the tools, I'd love to hear how things went. If you're thinking about trying one or two, I'm happy to answer your questions about how to make the best use of any of them. In either case contact me via my website, carlosvdapena.com, and click on the "Contact Carlos" tab in the upper right. While you're there, check out my blog posts, video blogs and other useful resources. Wishing you productive collaboration!

CHANGEMAKERS
BOOKS

TRANSFORMATION

Transform your life, transform your world - Changemakers
Books publishes for individuals committed to transforming their
lives and transforming the world. Our readers seek to become
positive, powerful agents of change. Changemakers Books
inform, inspire, and provide practical wisdom and skills to
empower us to write the next chapter of humanity's future.
If you have enjoyed this book, why not tell other readers by
posting a review on your preferred book site.

The *Resilience* Series

The Resilience Series is a collaborative effort by the authors of Changemakers Books in response to the 2020 coronavirus epidemic. Each concise volume offers expert advice and practical exercises for mastering specific skills and abilities. Our intention is that by strengthening your resilience, you can better survive and even thrive in a time of crisis.

Resilience: Adapt and Plan for the New Abnormal of the COVID-19 Coronavirus Pandemic
by Gleb Tsipursky

COVID-19 has demonstrated clearly that businesses, nonprofits, individuals, and governments are terrible at dealing effectively with large-scale disasters that take the form of slow-moving trainwrecks. Using cutting-edge research in cognitive neuroscience and behavioral economics on dangerous judgment errors (cognitive biases), this book first explains why we respond so poorly to slow-moving, high-impact, and long-term crises. Next, the book shares research-based strategies for how organizations and individuals can adapt effectively to the new abnormal of the COVID-19 pandemic and similar disasters. Finally, it shows how to develop an effective strategic plan and make the best major decisions in the context of the uncertainty and ambiguity brought about by COVID-19 and other slow-moving large-scale catastrophes. The author, a cognitive neuroscientist and behavioral economist and CEO of the consulting, coaching, and training firm Disaster Avoidance Experts, combines research-based strategies with real-life stories from his business and nonprofit clients as they adapt to the pandemic.

Resilience: Aging with Vision, Hope and Courage in a Time of Crisis
by John C. Robinson

This book is for those over 65 wrestling with fear, despair, insecurity, and loneliness in these frightening times. A blend of psychology, self-help, and spirituality, it's meant for all who hunger for facts, respect, compassion, and meaningful resources to light their path ahead. The 74-year old author's goal is to move readers from fear and paralysis to growth and engagement: "Acknowledging the inspiring resilience and wisdom of our hard-won maturity, I invite you on a personal journey of transformation and renewal into a new consciousness and a new world."

Resilience: Connecting with Nature in a Time of Crisis
by Melanie Choukas-Bradley

Nature is one of the best medicines for difficult times. An intimate awareness of the natural world, even within the city, can calm anxieties and help create healthy perspectives. This book will inspire and guide you as you deal with the current crisis, or any personal or worldly distress. The author is a naturalist and certified forest therapy guide who leads nature and forest bathing walks for many organizations in Washington, DC and the American West. Learn from her the Japanese art of "forest bathing": how to tune in to the beauty and wonder around you with all your senses, even if your current sphere is a tree outside the window or a wild backyard. Discover how you can become a backyard naturalist, learning about the trees, wildflowers, birds and animals near your home. Nature immersion during stressful times can bring comfort and joy as well as opportunities for personal growth, expanded vision and transformation.

Resilience: Going Within in a Time of Crisis
by P.T. Mistlberger

During a time of crisis, we are presented with something of a fork in the road; we either look within and examine ourselves, or engage in distractions and go back to sleep. This book is intended to be a companion for men and women dedicated to their inner journey. Written by the author of seven books and founder of several personal growth communities and esoteric schools, each chapter offers different paths for exploring your spiritual frontier: advanced meditation techniques, shadow work, conscious relating, dream work, solo retreats, and more. In traversing these challenging times, let this book be your guide.

Resilience: Grow Stronger in a Time of Crisis
by Linda Ferguson

Many of us have wondered how we would respond in the midst of a crisis. You hope that difficult times could bring out the best in you. Some become stronger, more resilient and more innovative under pressure. You hope that you will too. But you are afraid that crisis may bring out your anxiety, your fears and your weakest communication. No one knows when the crisis will pass and things will get better. That's out of your hands. But *you* can get better. All it takes is an understanding of how human beings function at their best, the willpower to make small changes in perception and behavior, and a vision of a future that is better than today. In the pages of this book, you will learn to create the conditions that allow your best self to show up and make a difference - for you and for others.

Resilience: Handling Anxiety in a Time of Crisis
by George Hofmann

It's a challenging time for people who experience anxiety, and even people who usually don't experience it are finding their moods are getting the better of them. Anxiety hits hard and its symptoms are unmistakable, but sometimes in the rush and confusion of uncertainty we miss those symptoms until it's too late. When things seem to be coming undone, it's still possible to recognize the onset of anxiety and act to prevent the worst of it. The simple steps taught in this book can help you overcome the turmoil.

Resilience: The Life-Saving Skill of Story
by Michelle Auerbach

Storytelling covers every skill we need in a crisis. We need to share information about how to be safe, about how to live together, about what to do and not do. We need to talk about what is going on in ways that keep us from freaking out. We need to change our behavior as a human race to save each other and ourselves. We need to imagine a possible future different from the present and work on how to get there. And we need to do it all without falling apart. This book will help people in any field and any walk of life to become better storytellers and immediately unleash the power to teach, learn, change, soothe, and create community to activate ourselves and the people around us.

Resilience: Navigating Loss in a Time of Crisis
by Jules De Vitto

This book explores the many forms of loss that can happen in times of crisis. These losses can range from loss of business, financial security, routine, structure to the deeper losses of meaning, purpose or identity. The author draws on her background in transpersonal psychology, integrating spiritual insights and mindfulness practices to take the reader on a journey in which to help them navigate the stages of uncertainty that follow loss. The book provides several practical activities, guided visualization and meditations to cultivate greater resilience, courage and strength and also explores the potential to find greater meaning and purpose through times of crisis.

Resilience: Virtually Speaking
Communicating When you can't Meet Face to Face
by Teresa Erickson and Tim Ward

To adapt to a world where you can't meet face to face - with air travel and conferences cancelled, teams working from home - leaders, experts, managers and professionals all need to master the skills of virtual communication. Written by the authors of *The Master Communicator's Handbook*, this book tells you how to create impact with your on-screen presence, use powerful language to motivate listening, and design compelling visuals. You will also learn techniques to prevent your audience from losing attention, to keep them engaged from start to finish, and to create a lasting impact.

Resilience: Virtual Teams
Holding the Centre when you can't Meet Face-to-Face
by Carlos Valdes-Dapena

In the face of the COVID-19 virus organizations large and small are shuttering offices and factories, requiring as much work as possible be done from peoples' homes. The book draws on the insights of the author's earlier book, *Lessons from Mars*, providing a set of the powerful tools and exercises developed within the

Mars Corporation to create high performance teams. These tools have been adapted for teams suddenly forced to work apart, in many cases for the first time. These simple secrets and tested techniques have been used by thousands of teams who know that creating a foundation of team identity and shared meaning makes them resilient, even in a time of crisis.